Birthday Diary

ISBN-13: 978-1719084062

ISBN-10: 1719084068

INTRODUCTION

It's obvious really, but this is how to use this book to record birthdays, anniversaries and any other notable dates that you need to remember. Here are a few examples:

January

1. A Friend (1974) — Birthday

   Remember to note the year of your friends birthday then you will be able to remember how old they are!

2.

3. Our kitten joined the family (2007)

4. My wedding anniversary (2003)

5.

   It is useful to note other dates that are important to you, not just birthdays and anniversaries

6. Moved into our house (2006)

January

1.

2.

3.

4.

5.

6.

7.

8.

January

- 9
- 10
- 11
- 12
- 13
- 14
- 15
- 16

January

17

18

19

20

21

22

23

24

January

25

26

27

28

29

30

31

February

1.

2.

3.

4.

5.

6.

7.

8.

February

- 9
- 10
- 11
- 12
- 13
- 14
- 15
- 16

February

17

18

19

20

21

22

23

24

February

25

26

27

28

29

March

1.
2.
3.
4.
5.
6.
7.
8.

March

9	
10	
11	
12	
13	
14	
15	
16	

March

17

18

19

20

21

22

23

24

March

25

26

27

28

29

30

31

April

1.

2.

3.

4.

5.

6.

7.

8.

April

9	
10	
11	
12	
13	
14	
15	
16	

April

17

18

19

20

21

22

23

24

April

25

26

27

28

29

30

May

1.

2.

3.

4.

5.

6.

7.

8.

May

9	
10	
11	
12	
13	
14	
15	
16	

May

17

18

19

20

21

22

23

24

May

25

26

27

28

29

30

31

June

1.

2.

3.

4.

5.

6.

7.

8.

June

- 9
- 10
- 11
- 12
- 13
- 14
- 15
- 16

June

17

18

19

20

21

22

23

24

June

25

26

27

28

29

30

July

1.

2.

3.

4.

5.

6.

7.

8.

July

9

10

11

12

13

14

15

16

July

17

18

19

20

21

22

23

24

July

25

26

27

28

29

30

31

August

1.

2.

3.

4.

5.

6.

7.

8.

August

9	
10	
11	
12	
13	
14	
15	
16	

August

17

18

19

20

21

22

23

24

August

25	
26	
27	
28	
29	
30	
31	

September

1.

2.

3.

4.

5.

6.

7.

8.

September

9	
10	
11	
12	
13	
14	
15	
16	

September

17

18

19

20

21

22

23

24

September

25

26

27

28

29

30

October

1.

2.

3.

4.

5.

6.

7.

8.

October

9

10

11

12

13

14

15

16

October

17	
18	
19	
20	
21	
22	
23	
24	

October

25

26

27

28

29

30

31

November

1.

2.

3.

4.

5.

6.

7.

8.

November

- 9
- 10
- 11
- 12
- 13
- 14
- 15
- 16

November

17	
18	
19	
20	
21	
22	
23	
24	

November

25	
26	
27	
28	
29	
30	

December

1.

2.

3.

4.

5.

6.

7.

8.

December

9

10

11

12

13

14

15

16

December

17

18

19

20

21

22

23

24

December

25

26

27

28

29

30

31

NOTES

NOTES

NOTES

NOTES

NOTES

NOTES

NOTES

Printed in Great Britain
by Amazon